BITCOIN OR BUST

Wall Street's Entry Into Cryptocurrency

Mark Helfman

INTRODUCTION

Depending on who you ask, bitcoin is either rat poison, an interesting technology, or a world-altering wonder-currency that will lead a revolution in finance and forever alter our contemporary notions of privacy, wealth, governance and security.

Some say it will liberate the masses from financial oppression and deprivation. Others claim it's a ponzi scheme destined to destroy all who participate in it.

Wall Street does not seem to care. It's happy to make money from those who want to buy it and those who want to bet against it.

Within the cryptocurrency community, many view Wall Street as a boon. They believe it will bring fresh money and enthusiasm to a flagging market. After all, U.S.-based investment companies hold $22 trillion in registered assets, plus much more in private accounts and off-shore funds. Without Wall Street's help, that money will never get into the crypto markets.

But is that really true? And if it is, will it work out the way people expect?

From late-2017 through 2019, traditional finance carved out a small foothold in the cryptocurrency market. CME opened bitcoin futures in December 2017 and several firms have applied for bitcoin ETF approvals. Intercontinental Exchange opened Bakkt, a massive, regulated, global cryptocurrency exchange for large investors and retail speculators. JP Morgan created its own cryptocurrency. NASDAQ spun up an exchange for digital assets.

Other firms followed suit. Fidelity, Sequoia, Goldman Sachs, and other Wall Street players built custody services, opened trading desks, and created subsidiaries focused on cryptocurrency products. Square, Robinhood, and smaller companies started selling cryptocurrency. Endowments and family offices reported small purchases of digital tokens and investments in blockchain start-ups. To date, VCs have closed at least $3.5 billion worth of deals with cryptocurrency projects and crypto-related businesses.

Does this mark the beginning of a shift of cryptocurrency away from bootstrapping developers and diehard believers towards professional money-makers? Will traditional finance rekindle the speculative frenzy that blasted cryptocurrency into mainstream discourse?

How will cryptocurrency change Wall Street?

More importantly, how will Wall Street change cryptocurrency?

In a series of articles from March to September 2019, I documented my thoughts on Wall Street's nascent efforts to enter crypto. These articles represent a snapshot in time but convey a message that remains pertinent and timely.

As bitcoin enters its next phase, traditional finance has a difficult decision to make: fight a technology that threatens to upend its business model or embrace an innovation that could unlock massive wealth (and with it, tremendous profits).

Its collective decision will have profound consequences for money, commerce, and the global financial system.

MARK HELFMAN

Mark Helfman is a *Medium* top writer worldwide for bitcoin and finance topics. He regularly appears among the most-viewed cryptocurrency writers on *Quora*, where his content has reached over 1.5 million readers in 2019 alone. He also contributes commentary and analysis for cryptocurrency and blockchain-related publications.

His book, *Consensusland: A Cryptocurrency Utopia*, explores the social, cultural, and financial challenges of a fictional country that runs on cryptocurrency. It sits on the Government Blockchain Association's recommended book list and received five-star ratings from Red Headed Book Lover and Readers' Favorite book review.

Previously, Mark worked for U.S. House Speaker Nancy Pelosi before joining H&R Block as a government relations professional. Those positions gave him an intimate look at how politics, money, and governance work in the real world. He also consulted for technology start-ups and owns small stakes in several early-stage businesses.

His insights on cryptocurrency reflect his understanding of history, politics, and economics from his experience in government, real estate, business, and private equity. He tries to keep it simple when he writes. It's cryptocurrency. Relax and enjoy the ride!

INSTITUTIONAL INVESTORS AND CRYPTOCURRENCY: BE CAREFUL WHAT YOU WISH FOR

February 2, 2019

If you listen to people in the cryptosphere, you'll hear a lot of chatter about "institutional investors," financial professionals who manage large investment funds.

Many people believe these investors will soon flood cryptocurrency markets with a tidal wave of money, bringing unimaginable wealth to all and saving cryptocurrency from its impending death.

Wall Street will bring its wares to Cryptocurrency Drive and soon we will see MOON, FOMO, and LAMBO (meaning, prices will go up a lot). Bitcoin will reach $1 million and **John McAfee won't have to eat his penis**. Salvation!

They say this money will start pouring in later this year when Fidelity begins to offer cryptocurrency products and Intercontinental Exchange opens Bakkt, a marketplace where huge institutional funds can move massive amounts of money from traditional markets into cryptocurrency.

NASDAQ could also have its first cryptocurrency products later this year. Börse Stuttgart launched its Bison trading app and announced plans to build a full-fledged cryptocurrency exchange. The Stock Exchange of Thailand will open its own digital asset marketplace.

All this on top of the smaller exchanges like Binance, Coinbase, and Gemini expanding their platforms to capture large investors and professional money managers.

As Morgan Stanley reported in a late-2018 summary of the investment industry's view of cryptocurrency, many institutional investors consider cryptocurrency a new asset class they can make money with. They understand the value of having a little cryptocurrency and they're encouraged by several studies showing average people generally interested in buying cryptocurrency but unsure of how to buy and scared of scammers. Most report their only concerns are regulatory and legal, not financial.

The interest is there. The only barrier is access and the perception of risk.

Wall Street is more than happy to knock down those barriers by providing safe, easy, regulated ways for large investors to buy cryptocurrency. In fact, Fidelity has already started educating its clients about cryptocurrency.

Hence the theory: once these traditional financial companies open their cryptocurrency platforms, lots of money will enter the cryptocurrency market. Up to $22 trillion in U.S.-registered investment funds alone, much more from abroad and unregistered accounts.

Mark, that's great news! What's the problem? We'll all make money!

Maybe, but I'm not sure it's going to work like you think it will.

Before I tell you why, let's step back and make sure we're all talking about the same thing here.

"Institutional investors" is a catch-all term for many different types of capital pools—endowments, commercial banks, mutual funds, hedge funds, pensions, trusts, family offices, etc. Different types of funds with different rules, strategies, risks, liabilities, and structures. Some will never want to buy cryptocurrency, others will never be allowed to buy it, and some have already bought a little.

Of the few who use these new investment platforms, most will either play the markets or store their cryptocurrency with the exchanges.

Yes, new money will go into the market, but it will also go out of the market.

These funds are run by professionals with an obligation to deliver the best returns for their clients. Those guys aren't going to make decisions based on a Twitter shill and HODL when the markets go down. They won't sit on a 500% gain because Reddit says the price is going higher.

They will study the projects they invest in, follow the markets, identify entrance points, and plan exit strategies. They'll hedge their bets with derivatives. They'll sell the bad projects before you hear the bad news and buy the good projects before you can get in. They'll find ways to wring profits from the markets, possibly at your expense.

Their job is to make as much money for their clients as possible. Most of them have a legal obligation to do so. They may appreciate cryptocurrency and believe in its potential, but that's a secondary motivation. Money is the driver here.

Of course, Mark. Wall Street is

greedy. Duh. Why is that a bad thing?

It's not greed that bothers me. It's not even Wall Street, specifically.

It's this obsession with institutional money. It's putting your faith and hopes in institutional money.

Investment institutions want to make money off of cryptocurrency, exchanges want to make money off investment institutions, and you exist solely to provide liquidity (somebody to buy their crypto so they can profit).

You may say "Mark, I already bought my crypto, I'm not going to fall into that trap. *I own the land, and they're coming for the gold! They're going to make me rich!*"

Maybe. Let's assume that's true.

What about your neighbor who's never bought cryptocurrency? He sees bitcoin go up 300% and hears all the chatter about how everybody's buying it and it's safe now and it's easy now and his investment advisor is telling him to put a few bucks in because he might just make a lot of money.

Who's looking out for him? Will you have the discipline to resist the texts from your friends and the media coverage telling you to buy after the pump? Will the cryptocurrency markets withstand the inevitable outpouring of scammers trying to make a quick buck off of people who don't know how cryptocurrency works? What will that do to the credibility of the cryptocurrency market? Of the governments that let cryptocurrency flourish, what will happen when the money runs out?

What happens when those big investors sell? When millions of people lose their money? Do you think people will say "welp, I gambled and lost, oh well, I take full responsibility for my actions" or do you think they'll say "I knew cryptocurrency was a scam, I can't believe I fell for it, and I'm never using it again."

All this focus on price and profits will delay the natural organic development of an innovative technology that has the potential to transform global commerce. Hype is the enemy of progress. It creates noise and distraction and keeps entrepreneurs and developers from testing, refining, developing their businesses and products. It always ends in disappointment.

Yes, cryptocurrency is a great speculation. But its value does not come from selling it to another person for more than you bought it for. Its value comes from actual usage.

I don't mean to come across as negative. I'm not — I understand this is a natural progression. More engagement and awareness is not necessarily a bad thing, and a lot of good could come from having this new money enter the cryptocurrency market.

While I'm selfishly happy to have institutional money pump the markets, I do not believe it's a sure thing.

Moreover, I worry about the average person.

I'm also worried about what happens to cryptocurrency once the new investing mania ends and I'm not thrilled about the idea of seeing big financial players making money off the greed and naiveté of uninformed people trying to get rich quick.

If that happens, Warren Buffet will be right in saying "bitcoin will end badly."

And you and I will be left holding the bag.

BAKKT WILL NOT SAVE CRYPTOCURRENCY (AND YOU WOULDN'T WANT IT TO)

March 22, 2019

Did you hear about Bakkt?

It's a massive, regulated, global cryptocurrency exchange built on the Microsoft Azure platform and managed by the same company that runs the New York Stock Exchange. When it opens, everybody who uses Bakkt will have a full suite of enterprise-grade investment services as well as the tools large investors need to properly manage funds. Most importantly, Bakkt will assume all the regulatory and operational risk of buying and selling cryptocurrency, including custody, security, insurance, and clearing for all transactions. Bakkt plans to open in 2019.

Why is this a big deal? Don't we already have cryptocurrency exchanges?

It's a big deal because no other exchanges have Bakkt's backing, expertise, trading infrastructure, and professional network. Its parent company, Intercontinental Exchange, owns some of the largest and most successful stock and commodity marketplaces in the world. People involved with Bakkt have decades of experience in traditional finance. Bakkt's backers include Horizon Ventures, M12, PayU, Pantera Capital, and Boston Consulting Group. Starbucks even signed a partnership.

In addition to ICE executives steeped in traditional markets, Bakkt's leadership includes alternative fintech pros Adam White (Coinbase) and Balaji Devarasetty (World Pay) along with several advisors from the cryptocurrency community. Bakkt has raised $182 million of investment capital and acquired Rosenthal Collins Group from Marex Spectron to improve its administrative operations.

Bakkt is about as legit as you can get.

This legitimacy goes a long way. With Bakkt, large investors won't worry about getting ripped off, seeing some scammer steal their money, dealing with low liquidity, or losing money when the exchange's owner dies. Plus, they have somebody to sue when things go wrong.

Fidelity, Boerse Stuttgart, TD Ameritrade, NASDAQ, Thailand's stock exchange, Switzerland's stock exchange, and other traditional financial entities already have moved into this space, but Bakkt draws all the attention because of its scope and pedigree— even though it hasn't opened yet.

In my previous post, I pointed out some reasons to worry about Bakkt and other traditional finance companies entering cryptocurrency. I'm cautious, not fearful, and it'll be interesting to see how everything plays out.

I can't fault Bakkt for filling a need. Wall Street needs a cryptocurrency marketplace and Bakkt fits the bill.

Bakkt will collect fees, big money will get a new playground, speculators will get an outlet for their spare change, traders will get a state-of-the-art trading platform, and financial professionals will get a new way to make commissions.

All this activity will make cryptocurrency seem regulated, professional, and normal. That's important because the public perception of cryptocurrency is that Bitconnect guy hyping a ponzi scheme.

Or, shirtless billionaire John McAfee holding a gun to his own head (Google it).

Bakkt meets a higher standard

With all due respect to Coinbase and Binance, those platforms can't meet the needs of financial professionals who manage institutional funds and large, actively-traded portfolios. These people need high-power computing, ultra-fast networking speeds, airtight custody, top-notch security, and lots of buyers and sellers. They're using sophisticated computers to manage large amounts of capital on behalf of big funds and wealthy people. They're not day-trading from their laptop using their blow money.

They demand higher standards. Bakkt plans to meet those standards.

Once it does, new professionals will enter the cryptocurrency markets—brokers, traders, money managers, and investment analysts working for large investment funds and money-movers.

These professionals will learn about cryptocurrency (some because they want to, others because their boss tells them they have to). They will share what they're doing with people at dinner parties, happy hours, board meetings, wherever. They will brag about their gains and might even laugh about their losses. They do this with every other asset, why wouldn't they do it with cryptocurrency?

Some will realize crypto is more than just bitcoin and a bunch of worthless, scam ICOs. Some will discover all the non-bitcoin cryptocurrencies that do more than just move money from one wallet to another. They will all feel comfortable about crypto. They will make others feel comfortable about crypto.

More importantly, these financial professionals will wear suits. They will have financial degrees and years of experience. They will project an image of credibility and savvy that you and I simply can't convey. They will educate their clients about technology, markets, projects, and profit potential. They will demystify cryptocurrency for people with lots of money.

Your uncle in finance will talk about how cryptocurrency is "safe" now. Financial advisors will suggest their clients invest 1% of their money into bitcoin "just in case it booms" (and take a small commission to do this for them). You'll hear more chatter about legitimate projects and real-life products that use cryptocurrency.

For the first time, cryptocurrency will have big-moneyed U.S. interests with established reputations, skin in the game, an interest in seeing prices go up, and a platform for making money when those prices go up. Bakkt is putting hundreds of millions of dollars into this effort. It's already hosting training and educational events. CEO of its parent company, ICE, told shareholders it's building a "moonshot" global cryptocurrency marketplace with plans to eventually move to a mass market. How long do you think they'll keep this news to themselves?

Once Bakkt has worked out the inevitable kinks and hiccups that come with every new venture, it will take its services to a mass audience. If this mass audience shows up, you're going to move from a small group of approximately 35 million people worldwide to a global base of 500 million people who already own some kind of financial instrument and many more who would buy from an app or service.

For those who claim the bubble burst and nobody will buy cryptocurrency again, did you know over one-third of Americans think cryptocurrency will grow and almost half would consider buying it? Extrapolate that to the rest of the world. There's your mass audience. That's a lot of people. And a lot of money.

Why do you think Google reversed its ban on crypto advertising to allow "regulated exchanges" but nobody else?

Mark, your headline said Bakkt will not save cryptocurrency. You just told me the opposite.

When did I say Bakkt will save cryptocurrency?

I didn't. I don't believe cryptocurrency needs to be saved. It just needs to be useful.

Bakkt doesn't care about that. It treats cryptocurrencies as assets and commodities, not solutions and networks. It builds financial vehicles rather than new economies. It creates crowds of chatterboxes rather than communities of users. It measures success in price growth, not token utility. It will feed a perception of cryptocurrency as a way to get rich, rather than a new way of solving social and economic problems.

Great for Wall Street. What does that do for you and me? What does that do for cryptocurrency?

Also, Bakkt creates a single authority over every transaction. It can stop, hold, freeze, and censor any activity within its ecosystem. Not to mention the security risk—one stolen password will undermine faith in the whole system, one hack and only God knows how much money will be lost. Cryptocurrency, *by design*, was created to prevent these very activities. Bakkt says it will take extra precautions to avoid this. We'll see.

On top of that, you have some big systemic risks if people start holding claims on other peoples' cryptocurrency. I'll spare you the technical details of how this works but you can read **this excellent letter to the U.S. Securities and Exchange Commission**. Here's my oversimplification:

> Most traditional financial products are based on some form of an IOU, sometimes with the same asset being promised to more than one person. Cryptocurrency does not allow IOUs.
>
> If you start letting people promise their cryptocurrency to another person, and let that other person promise cryptocurrency to yet another person, and so on, you create a series of claims. Each claim gets counted on a balance sheet.

For the system to work, each claim depends on the previous claim getting settled. What happens when people don't have enough cryptocurrency to settle those claims? What if the value of cryptocurrency falls to the point they'll never be able to settle those claims?

In traditional markets, you deal in paper, sometimes without actual assets exchanging hands and with strong regulatory safeguards against systemic collapse. Even then, you have an ever-present risk of catastrophe. With crypto, you have an actual asset and a patchwork of inconsistent regulations. A few bad deals could destroy the market.

Former Morgan Stanley executive Caitlin Long presents a technical discussion of this phenomenon in **How Wall Street Will Ruin Bitcoin**. Bakkt says it will not allow the types of activities she warns against. We'll see.

I also wonder about how Bakkt will change the regulatory debate in the U.S., where I live.

As a civil servant and former Congressional aide, I understand the importance of inertia when making policy. It's hard enough to get people motivated to create new rules. It's even harder to change those rules once you start moving in a certain direction.

What if regulators get enamored with Bakkt? Will they tilt regulations towards Wall Street? Will we end up with rules crafted for big players who care only about the money, not the technology? Will they see Wall Street as a necessary gatekeeper for people who want to use cryptocurrency—a sort of "tollbooth" regulating the cryptocurrency market?

Once you move in any direction, you get entrenchment, e.g., policymakers justifying their decisions, powerful interests defending their turf, a cohort of voters and legislators defending the new status quo because it benefits them. That's hard to break.

Bakkt says it won't get into politics. We'll see.

Mark, you don't want institutions to pump money into the cryptocurrency market?

I never said that. I said Bakkt will not save cryptocurrency.

First, we don't know how much money will really come into the cryptocurrency markets. Some money will certainly enter, but how long will it stay? When will it leave?

Second, let's assume people use Bakkt. What happens after new investors pump up the price of cryptocurrency and hype/shill until everybody's favorite coin reaches the moon and we all buy lambos? When Wall Street decides it's made enough money? When big investors lose interest? When the new money runs out? What will happen to the market?

Cryptocurrency does not need institutional money. It just needs people to continue developing its utility as a secure, global way for strangers to exchange things with each other and build businesses.

That development is already happening. During 2018, when prices collapsed, we saw 900+ VC partnerships, 100,000+ new jobs, massive private transfers of bitcoin, tremendous development, lots of new projects, several new investment platforms, corporate implementations of blockchain technology, business usage of cryptocurrency, and the creation of several operational cryptocurrency networks with actual business and expanding user bases.

This is progress, experimentation, growth, and traction. I'd hate for Wall Street to screw it up.

If cryptocurrency succeeds, it won't be because big investors make money speculating on their favorite coins. *For cryptocurrency to succeed, it cannot remain a speculation.* It needs to show results. It needs developers to continue improving cryptocurrency tools and technology, as they've been doing without Wall Street's involvement.

Wall Street doesn't bring results. It brings money and hype. It has already controlled the narrative of the bear market—"HODL because institutional investors are coming!"—without even having a platform to shill from.

With Bakkt, it will have that platform. Who do you think will control the narrative when the bull market begins?

You don't need Wall Street. You don't need institutions.

You need patience.

BAKKT WILL NOT SAVE CRYPTOCURRENCY.
IT WILL SAVE
WALL STREET

April 19, 2019

Rumors are swirling that Bakkt will pause its pursuit of U.S. government approval while it applies for a state-level cryptocurrency license.

Some say this means Bakkt is dead. I doubt it, but it doesn't matter. As I said before, Bakkt will not save cryptocurrency (and you wouldn't want it to). Cryptocurrency is developing slowly, naturally, and organically without Bakkt.

Bakkt won't save cryptocurrency. It will save Wall Street.

How will Bakkt save Wall Street?

Bakkt is interesting because it allows financial professionals to buy, sell, and trade cryptocurrency using an enterprise-grade trading infrastructure tailored for the unique demands of crypto traders. Like Coinbase on steroids, with derivatives, investment services, and the sophisticated tools large investors need to properly manage funds.

Most importantly, Bakkt will assume all the regulatory and operational risk of buying and selling cryptocurrencies, including custody, security, insurance, and clearing for all transactions.

Basically, Bakkt enables institutions and large investors to "safely" transact with clear rules, regulations, and expectations.

At some point, it will offer merchant solutions like credit cards and payment processing. Bakkt is building its entire marketplace from the ground up with one goal: dominate the cryptocurrency markets, just like its sister company the New York Stock Exchange dominates the equity markets.

If you've used cryptocurrency, you'll realize Bakkt is completely unnecessary and redundant. You need Wall Street when you buy a stock, clear a trade, purchase a CDO, or deal in derivatives and other financial products. You need a brokerage. You need a dealer. You need an investment company. You need somebody on the inside.

Downloading a bitcoin wallet? Anybody can do that. Signing up for Coinbase or Gemini? Easy. If you can learn how to use a checkbook, you can learn how to use a bitcoin wallet. If you can learn how to order food online, you can learn how to register for a cryptocurrency exchange. You don't need Wall Street.

That's the whole point of cryptocurrency: *anybody can use it.*

Is Wall Street important?

Yes, absolutely. It plays a vital role in the world's economy. It collects small amounts of money from many people and puts that money into big funds. Governments, businesses, farmers, and banks use those funds to grow, make money, and create jobs. Investors get a small reward for letting Wall Street do this.

In return, Wall Street takes a small profit and makes sure everybody gets a fair deal. Clearinghouses, settlement companies, recordkeepers, compliance professionals, traders, brokers, and many others get a cut of the action.

This is actually how Wall Street started. In 1792, U.S. equity markets were horribly disorganized and rife with fraud. A group of traders cemented an agreement in a house on Wall Street to deal only with each other using fixed, transparent fees. They set up small businesses around Wall Street to help them with settlement, clearing, certification, notarization, and all the legal and administrative activities that go along with an orderly, effective operation.

Over time, it grew into the U.S.'s financial center—and for financial institutions, a massive profit center.

Crypto kills profits

Cryptocurrency makes Wall Street's services obsolete.

You won't need clearinghouses once assets get tokenized and recorded on a blockchain. You won't need broker-dealers once developers create user-friendly smart contracts and decentralized exchanges. You won't need trading companies once distributed financial apps gain traction.

You will no longer need Wall Street for legal and administrative services like clearing, processing, certifying, and brokering your financial transactions.

You may not need Wall Street at all.

Finance as a whole could move to an AirBNB-like network of professionals and small companies connected by technology. You're already seeing a movement in FinTech away from clunky, bureaucratic firms to more nimble competitors like Personal Capital, SoFi, Circle, and other upstarts (some of whom are subsidiaries of Wall Street firms).

Cryptocurrency will speed up that trend.

Bakkt is Wall Street's best hope to keep its profits

Bakkt can't change this trend, but it can get ahead of it.

It can incubate the technologies that make smart contracts more useful. It can nurture the networks that connect entrepreneurs and cryptocurrency companies. It can develop the infrastructure needed to support mass adoption of cryptocurrency. It can use its image and credibility to build public faith in the legitimacy of cryptocurrency.

Bakkt is led by some of the most well-connected, established players in the world. It has the support of some of the biggest crypto advocates on earth. It has a bold vision and strong partnerships. It has the attention of the entire cryptocurrency market. It has the attention of the entire world.

Will it succeed?

For Wall Street's sake, it needs to. Otherwise, Wall Street will disappear.

ONCE WALL STREET STARTS TELLING ITS STORY, EVERYTHING ABOUT CRYPTOCURRENCY WILL CHANGE

June 28, 2019

News flash: this past Tuesday, U.S. regulators approved the first physically-delivered bitcoin futures contract for LedgerX, a highly-regarded bitcoin derivatives exchange.

This comes on the heels of TP ICAP, the world's largest inter-dealer broker, trading bitcoin futures on behalf of its clients and Bakkt nearing a now-inevitable opening.

If you didn't hear about any of this, it's ok. Most people missed it.

When you're in full-FOMO over a $13,000 bitcoin, that's what the news is going to focus on. It's certainly the obsession of Crypto Twitter and Reddit.

I have no qualms about hyping a bitcoin moonshot, but this news is far more consequential—not just for the blockchain industry, but also for your long-term chances of getting rich from cryptocurrency.

Hello, Wall Street. Welcome to crypto!

Fidelity was the first traditional Wall Street institution to create a cryptocurrency platform for institutional investors. TD Ameritrade, E*Trade, and Bakkt plan to follow. Rumors suggest NASDAQ plans to enter the space soon, too (it already has crypto indices and data platforms for institutional investors, as well as a subsidiary trading platform for security tokens).

If you think this means massive amounts of money are about to flow into crypto markets, you may be right. But I'd caution against getting wrapped up in the "institutional investors will send prices to the moon!" narrative.

That may (will?) happen, but there's a larger story you need to pay attention to.

Here come the professional money-makers

Look at the landing page for Fidelity's cryptocurrency services:

Screenshot of Fidelity's crypto page on June 26, 2019. https://www.fidelitydigitalassets.com/

What do you notice?

No mention of bitcoin, cryptocurrency, or prices. Sleek display with clean lines and muted colors. Words like "news" and "perspective." Opinions that are framed as facts and sprinkled with data.

This is the epitome of professional marketing content. It's everything I learned in political and business communication—skills and knowledge I apply at my day job (and fortunately can ignore when I blog).

Now read this excerpt from its bitcoin primer:

Bitcoin primer

Learn how this digital currency works, plus some risks to consider.

FIDELITY ACTIVE INVESTOR – 02/05/2019 · 7 MIN READ

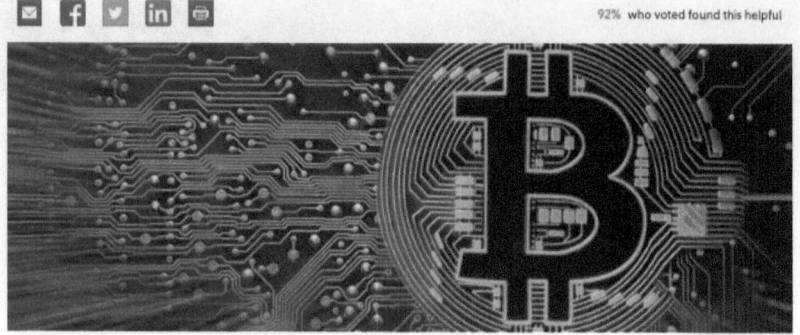

Key takeaways

- ✓ Digital currencies like Bitcoin are different from traditional forms of payment.
- ✓ There are benefits and significant risks associated with digital currencies.

What exactly is Bitcoin, and what are the risks involved in using it as a form of payment or as an investment opportunity? Here are some answers to frequently asked questions:

What is Bitcoin?

Bitcoin is the first and largest asset in the growing category of cryptocurrency (also known as digital currency). It was originally intended as a medium of exchange that is created and held electronically. Bitcoin was the first, but there are hundreds of digital currencies.

We'll focus on Bitcoin here to illustrate how digital currencies work. However, the underlying blockchain technology and functionality of Bitcoin are similar to many of the other widely used digital currencies, including Ethereum, Bitcoin Cash, and Litecoin. (For more on blockchain, see below.)

Excerpt from Fidelity's bitcoin primer on February 5, 2019.

https://www.fidelity.com/viewpoints/active-investor/beyond-bitcoin

What do you notice?

A well-written, balanced explanation of a new, potentially lucrative asset class. Read the whole thing on Fidelity's website.

Contrast those websites with bitcoin Reddit:

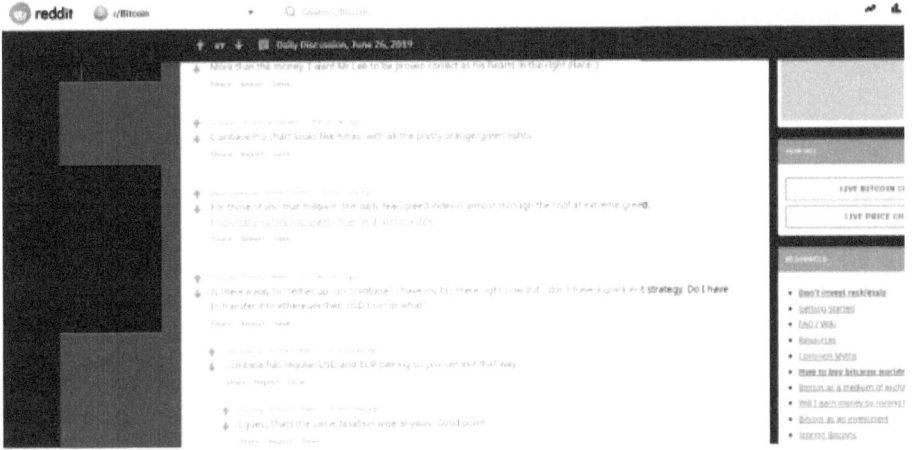

Bitcoin Reddit on June 26, 2019.
https://www.reddit.com/r/Bitcoin/

If you're young and cool, you're probably scratching your head like "what's the difference?" You may even like the Reddit feed better than anything Fidelity put out.

Wall Street doesn't care about you. It cares about your parents, grandparents, investment funds, and portfolio managers—people who have a lot more money than you (and care about it a lot more more than you do).

These people do not take advice from a random Reddit thread.

Suits, not lawsuits

As a digital native, you probably have no problem with the messy, personal content you read on the internet. It's unprofessional, zany, informal, and haphazard—usually posted on a bulletin board or blog that's cluttered with ads, links, and images.

Wall Street's money comes from people who are not digital natives. Your average millionaire is 61 years old, your average stockholder is 56 years old, and your average portfolio manager is 49 years old.

For the most part, these people don't want messy, personal information from random bloggers and outrageous internet personalities. They want professional advice from mature experts with experience, perspective, and demonstrated history of success.

They have money and obligations.

For individual investors, it's things like medical expenses, estate plans, businesses, and annuities. For pensions, endowments, and investment funds, it's usually rules that prevent holding risky investments of any kind.

Few will buy a speculative asset like bitcoin. In fact, they're probably more likely to sue their advisor for buying some.

As a result, Wall Street can't make a lot of money offering cryptocurrency-related services to these people (even if John McAfee says bitcoin will hit $1 million by the end of 2020).

Yes, Wall Street can collect some fees and commissions from smaller investors or funds that want to buy a little crypto, but that's not enough money to fund the massive investments in security, marketing, operations, and regulatory compliance necessary to bring cryptocurrency to the masses.

Unless...

Wall Street can change people's perceptions

From a pure investment standpoint, bitcoin shares the qualities of gold, oil, and many other commodities—violent swings in price over the short run, with no correlation to anything going on in the stock or bond markets.

For that reason, most managed portfolios include some of these types of commodities. In fact, if you believe in the Nobel Prize-winning investment approach called modern portfolio theory, you *must* own some. That's why Yale, Harvard, MIT, several pensions, and the Rockefeller family already have a little crypto in their portfolios.

It's ok for bitcoin to be speculative and wild.

It's not ok for bitcoin to be fake, useless internet money, as it's commonly perceived.

A few positive TV segments and mainstream news articles won't change that perception, but what about a sustained, multi-year marketing and communication effort by large, established Wall Street brands?

That just might.

Fortunately, Wall Street is great at that.

Winning hearts and minds

Fifty years ago, stocks were considered risky bets, basically gambling for rich people.

Then Wall Street created mutual funds, diversified portfolios, and tax-sheltered investment accounts. Stocks became safe, long-term investments.

Now, many people entrust their entire retirement to the stock market. Pensions put a big share of their funds in equities. Even some banks and annuity companies hold stocks as reserves.

Wall Street changed the narrative.

Thirty years ago, commodities were considered a playground for traders and speculators, not suitable for a legitimate investment portfolio.

Then Wall Street created ETFs as a convenient way to "gain exposure" to commodity prices. Commodities became "alternative assets" you could sell on-demand whenever the prices went up.

Now, commodity ETFs are part of almost every investment portfolio. Once unthinkable, now standard.

Wall Street changed the narrative.

Ten years ago, the world economy was in ruins, largely because Wall Street moved trillions of dollars into risky investments thinking they were safe. Protests and demonstrations broke out all over the world. U.S. government had to give banks and investment institutions $5 trillion to keep the financial system from collapsing.

Then, Wall Street booked record profits from a bull market that's lasted for over a decade (largely thanks to that $5 trillion handout).

Now, everybody's gloating about a strong stock market, well-capitalized banks, and surging financial companies. One major political party now advocates for *less* oversight and *fewer* restrictions on Wall Street while the other grudgingly (quietly) goes along.

Wall Street changed the narrative.

Rinse and repeat with crypto

Once Wall Street gets its feet wet with crypto, they'll say "hey, remember 2017? The markets were awash with scams and frauds. We came in and cleaned the place up. It's safe now. Buy bitcoin (but buy it from us, not Coinbase, **you** can't trust them)."

Wall Street will do this because it needs to. It's the only way to get that flood of money necessary to build out products and services for cryptocurrency investors.

If this seems hypothetical, look back at the Fidelity snippets I shared above. Now check out the websites for cryptocurrency businesses Bakkt, ErisX, and Circle (all subsidiaries of Wall Street firms).

Slick, clean, polished, well-written—and very pro-crypto.

Wall Street is planting the seeds.

Why you should care

Wall Street has a lot of money and power. Once it gets into the cryptocurrency markets, it will probably use this money and power for influence—marketing, lobbying, and networking.

At that point, everything will change.

Maybe it will ask your government to force you to use an "authorized entity" to hold your crypto instead of letting you hold your own cryptocurrency in your own wallets. That authorized entity would have to meet certain requirements—requirements that only a Wall Street firm could meet. After all, we can't let bitcoin fall into the hands of criminals and terrorists, right?

Or it might lobby for governments to allow the commingling of cryptocurrency with other assets. This is common with paper assets because it lets Wall Street create new financial products—i.e., new ways to make money—but it introduces massive risks for cryptocurrency markets (for reasons not worth getting into here).

Maybe Wall Street will get the U.S. government to give it sole control over airdrops, ICOs, STOs, IEOs, and other activities that result in new cryptocurrency? Perhaps it will even shut out normal people from getting in on these offerings, like it has shut average Americans out of private equity markets.

Or, maybe, Wall Street will try to control access to cryptocurrency like telecommunications companies control access to the internet under the guise of promoting innovation. Imagine new laws that let Bakkt or Fidelity serve as your "cryptocurrency service provider?"

It's possible Wall Street firms will buy up all the small cryptocurrency exchanges and custodial wallet providers, integrating them into new payment networks while shutting out light wallets. No more private keys.

And what happens when Bakkt sets up a node on the Lightning Network?

Wall Street talks, people listen

You may hate Wall Street, but you can't deny its influence. Your mom will never open a Coinbase account, but she'll let her financial advisor buy $100 worth of a bitcoin ETF "just in case" it booms.

Once people start to trust Wall Street with their crypto, Wall Street will try to make money off of their trust. Then they'll look for ways to protect and grow the power that comes from earning people's trust.

It's just what they do. I've seen this time and time again. So have you.

Frankly, we don't know how any of this will play out. Having worked on Capitol Hill, I know every big special interest has another big special interest trying to stop it from getting what it wants. Maybe Wall Street gets cut off and remains a marginal player in the cryptocurrency markets?

Maybe, but I doubt it.

Wall Street has a big voice, hordes of lobbyists, and well-connected advocates all over the world. It knows how to tell a compelling story and has all the money it needs to buy advertisements and positive PR (I guestimate $2+ billion based on a hodge-podge of marketing industry data).

Now, it has another way to line its pockets with your money.

Are you ready for that?

BITCOIN ETF WILL CHANGE THE GAME, BUT NOT THE WAY YOU'RE THINKING

July 26, 2019

Seems like nobody's talking about a bitcoin ETF anymore, but they really should. It's a true game-changer and destined to happen sooner than later.

Several Wall Street firms have asked for permission to create one and U.S. regulators will approve at least one of them eventually.

Once regulators approve a bitcoin ETF, they will cement bitcoin's legacy as a legitimate asset and open the floodgates for passive investors to pour money into bitcoin, leading to a boom in price and mainstream adoption.

At least, that's what people say.

Will you consider an alternative viewpoint?

In my book, *Consensusland*, cryptocurrency is just what you use when you need to buy something. One type of cryptocurrency for day-to-day business, another for international shipping, another for lending, etc. The idea of buying cryptocurrency as an investment seems odd. Why would anybody want to do that?

This is probably how you think about national currencies.

When's the last time you Googled the price of a kyat or wondered whether it's a good time to buy yen? Have you ever charted the price of the US dollar against the Saudi riyal? When has CNBC run a segment on how much the Turkish lira has dropped since 2014?

Bitcoin is really just another currency. Even the U.S. Securities and Exchange Commission says so. It's the unit of account for bitcoin's payment network.

Mark, what does that have to do with a Bitcoin ETF?

Perspective. It's all about perspective.

We have ETFs for many currencies—euros, Swiss francs, pounds, reals, pesos, and many more. Some ETFs go long, some go short, and some simply index.

I'm certain you have *never* bought any of those ETFs. They're for investors who want to speculate on foreign currency prices without actually holding foreign currency.

You could do that yourself, but it's complicated and expensive. In the U.S., exchange fees run as high as 10% or more for common currencies, higher for rare currencies. People in your country probably don't have foreign currency they're willing to sell to you. You also need to learn how to report it on your taxes. And anyway, where will you stash your foreign cash?

ETF managers usually have connections or other advantages that let them buy, sell, and store foreign currency more cheaply and easily than you could.

You pay a small fee to let them do that for you, as opposed to a big fee to do it yourself. You never actually touch the currency, you don't have extra paperwork, and you can sell whenever you want.

Meanwhile, your ETF manager takes a fee for offering this convenience. Everybody wins.

Bitcoin does not have any of those problems. It's easy to get—you only need to download a wallet and tap a few buttons. It's easy to sell—many wallets come with a built-in exchange.

It costs almost nothing to buy bitcoin from an exchange or wallet provider. You can store your bitcoin anywhere—even on a piece of paper.

Better still, you get to own your own bitcoin and use it however you want. With a bitcoin ETF, you don't own your bitcoin, the ETF does.

There is no need for anybody to use a bitcoin ETF.

If you have 15 minutes and a computer, you can do it yourself.

If there's no need for a bitcoin ETF, why do Wall Street firms keep trying to create one?

So they can make money.

They know people are interested in bitcoin. They knew it before this most recent pump in bitcoin's price.

Investment advisors reported getting constant requests from clients asking to put some of their money into bitcoin. A 2018 survey of financial professionals showed institutional concerns were regulatory and legal, not financial. Even during the dark days of the 2018 crypto collapse, U.S. interest in bitcoin was growing and I've heard it has grown in other countries, too. Fidelity published a primer on bitcoin and CNBC covers it often. Even *60 Minutes* ran a segment on it.

A portion of investors, money managers, and rich people want to gamble on bitcoin, they just don't want to deal with wallets, security, and storage.

For a small commission or a modest fee, Wall Street will take all that hassle and risk away. It can't do that when you buy and sell bitcoin yourself.

Bitcoin in every investment portfolio

Once the SEC approves a bitcoin ETF, it will end up a small part of all professionally-managed aggressive investment portfolios and many DIY investor portfolios. Bitcoin's a non-correlated asset that sometimes booms and keeping a small portion of your wealth in a bitcoin ETF is an easy way to make money off of bitcoin without having to do KYC/AML, set up a wallet, protect your private key, or worry about somebody scamming you.

For example, you put 1% of your money in the ETF and next time it booms, you can take some profits.

If it all goes to zero, you don't worry about losing 1% or less of your portfolio. You can lose that much in the stock market any given week (sometimes in a day).

And, unlike ETFs that speculate on boring things like wheat and nickel and collateralized debt obligations, bitcoin's ETF will attract casual investors who will "throw a few shekels" into it just because they heard from a friend or saw on the news that bitcoin's price is going up.

In other words, an ETF will bring in a lot of money from people who wouldn't normally care about bitcoin. Not a lot for them, but a lot for bitcoin.

Like pouring a pint glass into a thimble

Bitcoin is a small asset, barely a fraction of a fraction of the world's wealth.

All the bitcoin in the world is worth about $180 billion as of this post. Global investment portfolios include about *$40 trillion* worth of assets, possibly double that amount. The U.S. alone has more than $22 trillion in assets held by registered investment institutions, which does not include personal wealth and foreign accounts.

If you charted bitcoin on a pie graph of the world's wealth, you wouldn't even see it (I tried).

I had to find another way to visualize it.

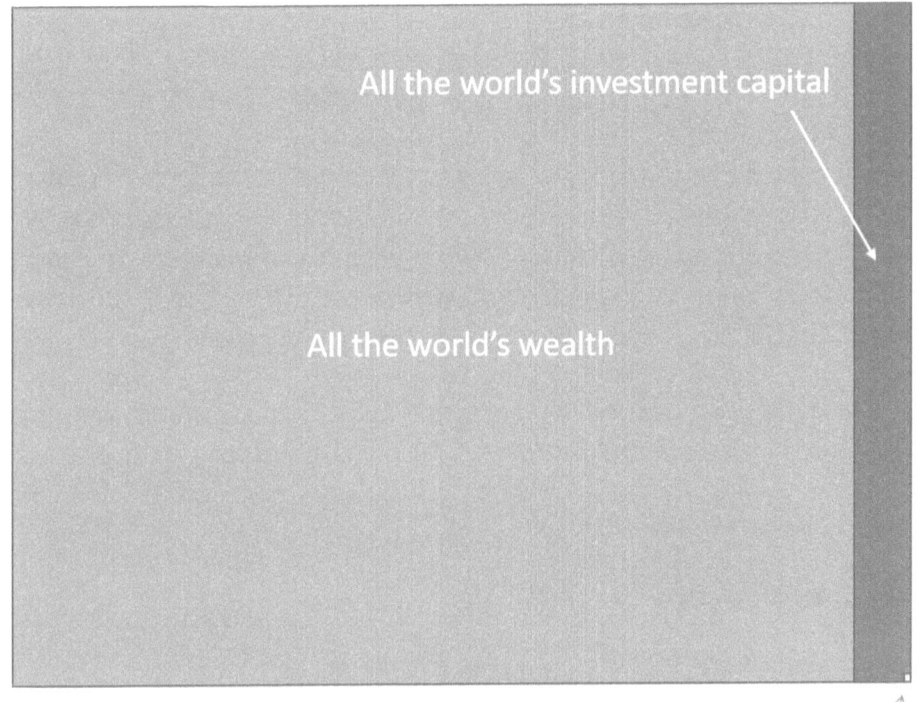

All the world's bitcoin

The rectangle represents the world's wealth (approximately $1 quadrillion). The dark blue strip represents the world's investment capital (roughly $40 trillion), and the yellow dot is bitcoin's slice of the pie.

Tiny.

A bitcoin ETF will be like scooping a pint glass into an Olympic-sized swimming pool and pouring it into a thimble. A tiny amount of water for the pool, but a deluge for the thimble.

Wait, Mark, that means bitcoin ETF will send prices to the moon!

That's the conventional wisdom. Gold doubled within three years of getting its first ETF, and it was a far more established (and much larger) asset than bitcoin.

Don't assume it will work that way. Copper tanked after its first ETF and still hasn't recovered. Some analysts say ETFs don't actually affect the price of their underlying commodities—markets still set prices and besides, if you weren't interested in bitcoin before the ETF, why would you be interested in it after?

It's hard to predict how high prices will go or how long the pump will last. New bull run? Another 2017-esque bitcoin mania?

Or a huge pump-and-dump?

An ETF makes it easy to move money into the markets ... *and out of the markets.*

Most buyers of ETFs will be financial professionals and experienced investors, people who know how to make money from investing. These guys will not sit on a 500% gain because a random YouTuber says to HODL. They won't buy after a 500% pump because somebody on CNBC says it will go higher. They study the markets, pick the best entries, and plot the best exits.

With an ETF, they can crash the markets as easily as they can pump the markets.

Also keep in mind, ETFs are a first-world investment instrument for well-connected or wealthy people. You can't expect massive amounts of people to buy into the ETF. Your average person has never heard of an ETF and doesn't know how to buy one, even if he or she had enough money to spare on the investment.

They're more likely to have heard of bitcoin, but less than half of one percent of the world owns even a single satoshi of bitcoin.

As far as having their portfolio manager put a little money into bitcoin? Most people don't have a portfolio at all, much less somebody managing it.

It's also possible ETF shares will cost too much for your average person. For example, one ETF proposal has a minimum share price of $200,000.

On top of that, consider how many people don't have access to financial products at all (in many countries, this is the norm). These people operate totally outside of a banking system and could never buy an ETF of any kind, much less bitcoin.

But let's assume bitcoin booms after the ETF opens. Average people will start buying because they hear you can make money from bitcoin and see the price going up.

They won't buy the ETF because they won't have a broker or investment account. Instead, they'll go to Coinbase or some other exchange to buy bitcoin directly. With no guidance and little understanding of bitcoin, these people will simply try to ride the wave higher, just like in 2017.

Once we get new highs and more publicity, those financial professionals and experienced investors will take some of their money out. It's just what they do. You might, too.

If we go full boom, the smart money will sell, quick—whether through the bitcoin ETF or a private broker or an exchange.

What about everybody else?

When that money leaves the market, who will be left to buy more bitcoin? How will bitcoin sustain its boom?

Wall Street will take its profits elsewhere. Brokers and dealers will chase the next big trend. ETF providers will stick around—if only to continue collecting fees from clients HODLing bitcoin for another boom that may never come.

Millions of people will lose money.

Wall Street always wins. A bitcoin ETF just makes it easier for them to do that.

PREPARE FOR A NEW WAVE OF ICOS FROM WALL STREET

September 13, 2019

Did you hear?

Blockstack's ICO raised $23 million, including $15.5 million through the first-ever U.S.-approved public token sale.

With YouNow following in its footsteps, you can expect more blockchain businesses to follow the path to U.S. regulatory approval.

Tokens for dollars—no bitcoin needed.

After years of failed attempts, companies can finally raise money for new cryptocurrency projects that comply with U.S. laws. And when you buy those cryptocurrencies, you won't risk your investments getting rekt by lawsuits.

This may seem like a boring, insignificant event, but it could change the nature of cryptocurrency in ways we can't imagine. It's also one more reason Binance's move to the U.S. is so brilliant —and much more consequential than simple regulatory compliance.

Power to the people?

Kudos to the U.S. Securities and Exchange Commission (SEC) for financial innovation. While it will need to clarify some details of its decision, it finally created a legal way to bring ICOs to the public.

Using Regulation A+, businesses can sell tokens to anybody, even those who do not fit SEC's definition of accredited investor. Instead of getting shares in the companies, investors will get tokens. Everybody can participate.

It's a whole new paradigm. Exciting!

But unless you're an expert in Regulation A+ and connected to everybody who would ever give you money, you need a broker or backer—almost always a Wall Street firm or a crowdfunding platform connected to Wall Street.

While this makes a lot of sense, it also gives Wall Street an interest in ICOs.

More specifically, an interest in *making money* from ICOs.

ICOs are dead. Long live ICOs!

Does it seem odd that Wall Street would care about ICOs?

In 2017, it called them scams. Worse than bitcoin. Even now, many ICOs are stuck in lawsuits, some have paid millions in damages, and a few ICO leaders sit in jail. Many have failed.

Yet only *now* does Wall Street get in the game?

Of course. It's all about opportunity.

In 2017, Wall Street had no way to make money from ICOs.

A bunch of scammers and a few legitimate businesses posted whitepapers and wallet addresses on the internet and made a shit-ton of money. Nobody knew what was legal or not. None of the ICOs had to register with anybody. A new ICO popped up seemingly every day. And they were all private, beyond the reach of the professional money-makers.

How could Wall Street get a cut of that action?

It couldn't.

Thanks to the SEC, Wall Street now has a safe, U.S.-regulated way to make money off of new token offerings. It can market them as SEC-compliant, fully vetted start-ups that offer tantalizing opportunities and novel technology with massive potential.

When you consider the perceived drop in IPOs and a never-ending stream of successful companies choosing to stay private for longer, ICOs come at a very opportune time. New businesses simply aren't going public like they used to, but crypto is booming.

Nobody makes a commission from a company that stays private.

Flipping an ICO? Could bring in a few bucks, maybe. At least until SEC approves a bitcoin ETF.

Buy the next bitcoin!

Why would an ICO use Wall Street when it can take its sale directly to the public? Especially when Binance has its own platform and U.S. doesn't have the friendliest crypto rules.

Wall Street offers some advantages.

It connects ICOs to regulators, networks of investors, and the general public. It has lawyers, consultants, advisors, and experts to support any new venture. It's easier to get support, approval, and exposure for your projects when you have these insiders and professionals on your team.

Also, Wall Street controls about a quarter of the world's wealth, mostly through banks and investment institutions that hold money and assets on behalf of pensions, families, annuity companies, endowments, and others. Without Wall Street's backing, ICOs have a tough time getting access to that money.

On top of that, Wall Street's involvement cuts a lot of risks. It's hard to structure an ICO that fits U.S. rules. If you screw up, you risk getting sued or shut down. Wall Street will try its best to make sure that doesn't happen.

Meanwhile, Wall Street gets to make money and advertise a chance to buy the next bitcoin (at least, a chance to make people *think* they're buying the next bitcoin).

Everybody wins.

Wall Street's big move or last stand?

Cryptocurrency has one key advantage over private equity and stocks:

Anybody can create, distribute, and exchange it any time, any place, with anybody they want, instantly and with certainty both sides get the result they expect.

Thank you, blockchain.

Unless a company needs U.S. citizens to buy its token, it has no need for Wall Street or the SEC. Even Blockstack was able to raise $7 million from non-U.S. investors—no small feat for an upstart tech project.

Wall Street may have lots of connections, but it doesn't have a monopoly on professional networks. Lawyers, advisors, consultants, traders, experts, and brokers can start their own businesses or find other non-Wall Street opportunities to ply their craft. On top of that, new financial and telecommunications technologies give these professionals access to each other (and financial markets) without the help of a Wall Street firm.

This will seem obvious when we get robust security token platforms and other blockchain-enabled financial innovations.

Once we get to that point, when anybody can offer any cryptocurrency on any terms with safety and integrity, we will not need a Wall Street entity or U.S. regulator to oversee the sale.

Wall Street knows this, too. Why do you think all those Goldman Sachs executives left for crypto-related ventures?

It will take a while for entrepreneurs and developers to wrap their heads around this monumental shift. Even longer to create the networks, processes, and technology to support this approach to finance. Government agencies will come last (they always play catch-up).

Now is the time for Wall Street to get ahead of those changes. Cornering the market on ICOs will help.

Playing the influence game

With a foothold on ICOs, how long will Wall Street wait before suggesting U.S. regulators put it in charge? After all, who else can you trust to make sure terrorists and scam artists won't use ICOs to enrich themselves?

When does Wall Street petition for sole domain over ICOs, IEOs, security tokens, and new blockchains?

Will Wall Street firms start buying out all the ICO platforms that spring up over the next decade? Or start their own?

Here's the story Wall Street will tell:

> Back in 2017, ICOs were scams and frauds. With our help, the government cleaned everything up. Now, you can safely buy your stake in the financial networks of the future. You won't need to set up a shady, complicated crypto wallet or worry about con-artists trying to pull an exit scam. You might even find the next bitcoin! We'll handle the paperwork. You just give us your money.
>
> —*Wall Street to everybody else*

That story is compelling and true.

Win before Binance (or somebody else) does

Wall Street needs to tell that story before Binance can do it. Not just because Binance is competition, but also because Binance represents a new generation of effective, competent, savvy, well-financed cryptocurrency investment platforms that Wall Street does not control.

As those platforms continue to succeed and grow, they will take Wall Street's turf.

Could they succeed if Wall Street lobbyists craft a regulatory environment designed to kill them? If Wall Street corners the market for ICOs? If Bakkt really succeeds the way everybody hopes?

It'll be interesting to see how it all unfolds.

Wall Street brings order and stability to every market it's involved in. That's not a bad thing. In fact, we may all benefit from Wall Street's involvement in ICOs. The Internet boomed once U.S. Congress handed it over to telecommunications companies.

But maybe not. Wall Street's mere presence may tilt the whole crypto market off-kilter—or at least skew the industry in favor of big, entrenched financial interests.

Or maybe blockchain's transparency and security may make Wall Street obsolete?

In any event, Wall Street continues to quietly creep into the crypto. Will this make things better or worse?

I would love to hear your thoughts. Tweet me **@mkhelfman** or email **mark@markhelfman.com**.